THE THINGS I WANT TO SAY

Kelly churchill

This book is for those who feel like they've been let down, those who have gone through silent battles, and not so silent ones. This is for those who feel like they can't voice how they feel.

These are the things that I wanted to say but couldn't, the things that were left between the lines of the things I did say. This is for little me, to prove to her that we got through it.

I encourage you to read this book however you want, from front to back, back to front, one page at a time, flick to a random page, whatever you fancy. There are no rules.

Look after yourself, stay safe and remember that you can do anything.

Acknowledgments

Thank you to:

Jess & Emily – The amazing super duo! Without these two I wouldn't be where I am today. Emily knows what I'm thinking before I even think it, and Jess likes to challenge my ridiculous self ideals. They have stood by me even when I have tried to push them away, and I will forever be grateful for having them help me even when I have been difficult to deal with.

Alex house team – Where do I start, this amazing group of people have truly changed my life. They've quite literally been there both day and night. From having a quick chat to the hours and hours of games I've made them play, to the drives and sitting with me while I cried. I wouldn't be half the person I am today without them.

And to my friends and family, in which there is not enough space to list you all. Thank you for everything you have done; we may not always get on (what family does?) but this would not have been possible without you all. I love you xx

Warnings

While I have tried to make this book as friendly as possible, some of these poems contain language that could be seen as triggering. I am asking you to please stay safe and look after yourself. Some topics mentioned include self harm, suicide, grief, trauma, and other symptoms surrounding mental health. I have tried to make these poems as kind as possible, and many are open to interpretation.

If you feel affected by these poems then please reach out to someone and talk it through. I encourage readers to take self care breaks and find some comfort in the fact that you are not alone.

Thank you for your support; I love and appreciate you.

Kelly x

Things I want to say

When I was younger
You bought us wooden toys
With wooden blocks
That fitted through the holes made for them in the lid
My brother spent hours
Making the cube fit the square hole
The triangle prism through the triangular hole
And no matter how hard he tried
None of the shapes could be forced to fit the wrong place
Maybe that should have taught you a lesson

I guessed you never had the same toy when you were younger
Because if you had you would have realised that I didn't fit
Into the future that you had envisioned before you ever met me
One with specific sides and dimensions
As if I was a wooden toy
And not a fucking person
As if I could be pushed and moulded until I was, at last
perfect
Exactly who you wanted
Exactly who you decided I was when you saw me for the first time

I see the way you love the sky and the stars that are scattered throughout space

Things I want to say

So why don't you love the thoughts making
constellations across the synapses in my brain
And if you can love the cratered moon then why can
you not love the holes in me too?
You see the beauty in dark autumn leaves and love the
way christmas lights
Light up the world
So why can't you see that beauty in me?
When you admire the sunrise or sunset
You don't wish for it to be quiet and be tame
So why do you wish that I'd do the same...

Things I want to say

Whenever he saw a traffic light all red lit up
He would always drive through it even though it
would only take one simple moment
To stop
Desperate to be destructive
He ignored my signs meaning no
I tell myself he's colour blind
Reds morph to greens
Giving him permission to go
I never imagined a two letter word would cause such
mayhem
Yet I'm not sure I can get over it
Not without learning to say them
Maybe I didn't object enough
Wasn't confident enough with the ability of my voice
But how could I ask my mouth to move
During an event that wasn't my choice

Things I want to say

So here I am once again
Packing all of my belongings
Into unusual, unorganised, unstable old boxes
And I hope this time will be my last
I think I need to take time to process all the things of
my past
I don't think I'll ever get used to this
All the unusual, unorganised, unstable old memories
I'll appreciate the good times that we had
But nothing lasts forever
And I know I can't get better
Sitting in this unusual, unorganised, unstable old
house
If I could, I'd drive a couple hours
Until I find myself and stable health
It's all I've ever wanted
All that I need
For this mind is suffocating
And I need to fix all the unusual, unorganised,
unstable in me

Things I want to say

It always hurts a little to come home
Like I'm trying on an old piece of clothing
That I've gotten too big for
Still familiar but pinches in most places
And I want to feel like I'm still me when I'm here
But I just don't quite fit anymore
And maybe deep down
I know I never did

Things I want to say

"I love you this much" I want to say as I pinch my
thumb and finger in front of my face
"Nothing can come between us" explains that lack of
space
You see
Meeting you was like meeting myself
But in a different hue
You're me but just that little bit lighter
"It feels like we've been friends forever" you turn to
me and say
"I know, it's mad" I reply
Thinking how lucky things have turned out this way
You're my best friend
My home away from home until the very end
It's like looking in a mirror but with a better view
We are the same but also so different
How did I become so lucky to have a best friend like
you?
Thank you for loving me when I cannot love myself
Thank you for the time you gave me a hand to hold
And the many many hours spent on the road
Thank you for the money, the food and the time
And sorry for all the shitty lines that don't quite
rhyme

I love you

Things I want to say

I know you're only human but stop using that as an
excuse
Cause I'm sick of being grateful for all that you put
me through
I had to mature way too fast
Because "life was hard"
And I know it wasn't your fault
And I know you tried your best
And I know that your heart felt lost inside your chest
But
I feel like I was your therapist
When I should have been allowed to feel things too
I feel like my time was robbed
I grew up viewing you to be everything I never want
to
Be
You spoke so loud but never listened
And I hope you're proud because there's a lot that
I'm missing
So yes
You tried your best
But can you please acknowledge that you're a mess
Because I can forgive
But my mind will not forget

Things I want to say

I am a "real adult"
I have my own flat with a postcode that is mine to
remember
And my parents live
what feels like a million miles away
But is only down the road
I have to make my own appointments
Buy my own food
Pay a hundred bills and
Clean all of the rooms
And while I've been doing all that for years now
Everything somehow feels harder
When you're on your own
I have a few friends who I think will stick around
But I've been wrong about that one before
And I have a few people who are there for me
Who always come banging on my door
So this is what growing up is
It feels
All at once
Too much
But not at all enough

Things I want to say

I noticed it getting bad again
when I considered 2 hours to be "good sleep"
I noticed it getting bad again
When I was drinking more coffee than I was water
I noticed it getting bad again when
There was more smoke in my lungs than oxygen
I noticed it getting bad again when
I had more calls than I did texts
I noticed it getting bad again when
The only thing dragging me out of bed was a packet of
pills
I was seeing what my body could handle
I mean what's the worst that could happen?
I die?...
That's how I noticed it getting bad again

Things I want to say

I'm trying to build this sturdy, happy life for myself
One where I try my best, correct my worst and put
everything into all the things I love
One where I forgive myself and this earth and those
who hurt me
I'm trying to build a life where I see the sun through
the clouds
Where I wake up earlier, go to bed earlier
One where I make the best memories
Give my time to the people I love
And to myself too
One where I set goals for myself and achieve them
One where I never feel the need to apologise for being
me
And I make boundaries
A life where I stop pouring from an empty cup
Take my time to fall but get back up
And I know you've probably heard it all before
Told to you by parents, doctors and teachers or
Like me, that person you met when you were just 21
And the world felt like it was crushing you
I'm just trying to build myself a sturdy, happy life
One that I'd be proud to describe to them now

Things I want to say

I always believed that everybody I love would grow
with age
But I guess I've come to realise that that's not always
true
Cause you said goodbye to us before your birthday
even arrived
And the seasons have continued to change
But you'll always be frozen in time
When the flowers grow
And the snow starts to fall
Will it hit me then that you have gone?
I guess the hardest part of growing up
Is that some of the people that you love can't

Things I want to say

Whoever said "grief gets easier over time" can
Respectfully
Lick the bottom of my left shoe
Because it's Friday tomorrow
And I hate the weekends
And all I wanna do is fall into our routine
Because it's been nearly 4 years since we got together
Nearly 3 since you left
And I still feel the pit in my stomach telling me to
grieve all over again
Because the weekends have never gone back to
normal
And I mean they were never normal to begin with
But now I don't get to wake you up
And fight over the covers
Because I thought I got through this part
Because I thought I'd got through all 7 stages
But maybe the steps got disorganised because I feel
upset (5)
And then in denial (2) all over again
Yesterday I felt that acceptance (7)
But today I can barely get through the day
Without the shock (1) and guilt (3) carving out my
chest
And this means that some stages (4 and 6) have
disappeared
So to whoever said grief gets easier with time
I would like to know what sort of watch you have
Because I think mine has gotten stuck
Maybe it does get easier with time

Things I want to say

Or maybe the thoughts get easier to dismiss
I don't know
But I do know that Friday is tomorrow
And I won't get to see you

Things I want to say

I feel like I continue walking straight into hell
Just to try to save you
I continue giving up all that I love
Just to try and help you
I have to learn it has done nothing
But break me into pieces

I was setting myself on fire
Just to try and earn your love
But now I'm here alone
Burning in this house
That I'm trying to make into a home

You light the matches
Then leave me on my own
With the flames that you watch grow
I feel like our memories are turning into ashes

I am made of glass
And you are the one who shatters me

Things I want to say

I'm running low on patience
My bones ache from growing pains
I'm starting to feel lost
Did I want to be found anyway?
I'm having to relearn how to direct
The connection that maybe didn't even exist in the
first place
How have we managed to take the wrong turning and
every right one?
We're going round in circles
And fuck, I am so dizzy
I am running out of patience
I'm holding on to every last memory of your being
Trying to follow them to
Whatever sick bond that we are sharing
I blinked and now the distance is so far from anything
I remember
I'm changing from who I was
And I've found the good in this
How did we get so far?
From being what we wanted to be
I don't think I ever really knew you
Because now I am changing into a different version of
lost
And I'd say I miss you
But you were never really there to begin with

Things I want to say

I tend to self destruct instead of cry
Ignore my feelings instead of feeling
Them
I'm a broken person
When you raise your voice my glass skin shatters
They say "you're trauma made you stronger"
But I made me stronger
They don't tell you about how they treated me
How if you push into my skin I dent
How my body is scarred from being exposed
To too much too soon
Turning me into therapist
I was still a person
But how dare I have the audacity to feel
Told myself to "put my big girl boots on
Chin up
Stop moaning"
Acting as though I was the glue that sticks everything
back together
Call me sellotape and paper
Sticking the ripped parts of people back together
Call me soap and sponge
Pressing myself up against the glass
To wash away the sins
Pretending I have no problems of my own
I've spent my life hiding pain
Treating cuts
Call me doctor
Treating disease
Call me vaccine

Things I want to say

Giving energy and relief
I walked around like nothing could take me down
All confidence and smiles
I was hiding from myself but it's caught up to me now
Throwing up trauma
Call me virus

Things I want to say

Controversial opinion but

Trauma did not make me stronger
Trauma made me traumatised
Trauma gave me flashbacks and no sleep
It gave me an alphabet of diagnosis and a dictionary
of medications
Trauma stole my childhood
And my teenage years
And the years between then and now

Trauma did not make me stronger
But it did give me some good skills
I can tell you who is walking down the stairs
Just from the sound of their footsteps
I can tell you what happened to someone that day
Just from the way they entered the house and closed
the door

Trauma did not make me stronger
Trauma did not give me a good sense of humour
I did
Because when I was confronted with my pain all I
knew to do was laugh
If I couldn't joke about the trauma
I do not want to know what would have become of me

Trauma did not make me stronger
But that is not to say that I am not strong
I am

Things I want to say

I am stronger than most people I have met
Trauma does not get to take the credit for that one
I do
The people who hurt me were not the ones who spent
hours with unspoken demons
I did
The events I can no longer think about for fear of
causing pain did not make a home out of me
I made one

Do not tell me that "all of this made you stronger"
Because I will tell you that I did that
I will tell you that the one thing more substantial than
the pain
Is my ability to keep looking for change over and
fucking over again
My abusers do not get the credit for the strength that
you see
I do
It's the one thing they cannot steal from me

Things I want to say

I remember the funeral like it was yesterday
When we arrived I was greeted by all our friends
Your family
The one that once was mine too
For a moment we forgot that you weren't there
Our common denominator
But our reality hit us
Once the music started playing and your picture came
up on that stupid fucking screen
I kept repeating to myself over and over
This is a mistake
Until all words had lost their meaning
I'm not sure at what point I started crying but when I
started I knew that I couldn't stop
When your finality was being defined
Your mum giving love and laughter to your life
Pain flew through the audience
All my senses stopped and it may have only been a
second but it felt like my body giving up
I had spent the month waiting for a reply from you
Telling me that this wasn't real
That you were still here
Waiting for me
I didn't have the luxury of denial anymore
It was one of the hardest moments of my life
How could we live in a world where your laughter
doesn't exist?
It's been almost 3 years since you left
There isn't a day that goes by where we don't all
think of you

Things I want to say

I know that wherever you are is where you chose to be
And I hope to god everyday that you found the peace
you were looking for
I still selfishly hope that you're waiting for me

Things I want to say

Nobody has apologised for the things they did to me
But they blame me for how I react
And leave me to fix the mess they created
All on my own

- Isn't it funny

Things I want to say

Every evening I go to couples therapy with my
trauma
It fills my head with "stay in bed" every morning
The nightmares press their way into my skull afraid
that I will leave them
After I scrape myself together
And look in the mirror
I still look like him
Like midnight flashbacks and daytime panic attacks
Our sessions are however long they last
And we spend that time
Going over the same things again and again
Hurt has been around pretty solidly for a couple
months
That means it's getting serious right?
The book asks if I've slept properly recently
Asks if I've left the flat recently
And I go silent
The answer is no
But I don't want to admit that
The book asks if anything has improved since I
started self harming again
I'm now forced into silence
The tablets and blades treat me well
They get me out of bed in the morning
Help me take a shower
Trauma threatened to bring in his friends pain and
anger
So I threatened to see even more of the others
All of them and all at once

Things I want to say

So I did
That's the night I ended up in the hospital
But that was only one time.. or 2.. or 3
So me and trauma spent some time together
The book thinks I'm only with him because my life is
just a little too fucked up
Or because I still sometimes wish I was anyone else
It doesn't understand this is the most loved I have
ever felt
We decide times up, same time tomorrow
Trauma whispers fine and slams the book closed
I'm making improvements
But that trauma and I will probably be together for
the rest of my life
But I'll be more independent soon
I've been starting to think more about that

Things I want to say

I think younger me would be disappointed
Because I watched the adults around me ruin
themselves
Searching for love in hateful places
Searching for warmth in bodies that weren't their
own
And I promised myself I wouldn't turn out like they
did
I wouldn't let myself get hurt by the same people who
claimed they loved me
I wouldn't look for warmth in anyone else but me
I didn't want to become someone who couldn't
separate what they needed
From what someone else wanted
And I promised myself I wouldn't stop searching
For laughter in the little moments
For happiness in the sunrises
For the good in bad people
I was so much better than that
I didn't want to lose my determination to participate
in life
I think I've slowly been forgetting that

Things I want to say

How did I go from a girl who so easily loved everyone
And everything
A girl who loved an early morning coffee
When the world was in that in between state of not
asleep
But not quite awake
A girl who loved to be outside feeling the breeze on
her skin
And the sun in her eyes
The girl who always had a something to be happy
about
Because she finally got what she wished for

To the girl who now hasn't tasted a coffee in weeks
A girl who just wants to stay in bed
A girl who hasn't seen the sun hit her eyes
But instead has made friends with the moon
Because sleep and early mornings and the wide awake
world are just too much for her

Where did that happy little girl go?
I really want her back
Because I hate who I've become now

Things I want to say

I was 6
And I lost my innocence

When I hear loud noises
I have a panic attack

I was 7,8,9
And trying to fix what you broke

When I have nightmares
I see your face

I was 10,11,12
When I had spoken to more professionals that I had
friends

When I smell that body spray
And my mind crumbles

I was 13,14,15
And my life was forever changing

When I think of my years
I can't think straight anymore

I was 16,17,18
And my life became mine

Things I want to say

I want to love
And be loved
I want my future to be better than my past
And my children to have a better start in life than I
did
I want my family to be proud of me
And say it
I want to drink iced coffee on a hot day
And iced coffee on a cold day
Sometimes I laugh at something I don't think anyone
else would laugh at
I still think about all the stupid things I said in high
school
And I still think about what could have been if the
things that had
Hadn't
Sometimes I think I care too much
And other times
Not enough
I'm just trying to do the right thing but I don't know
what that is
I just make it up each day

Things I want to say

When I am asleep the monster is there
When I am awake the monster is still there
The image is not as clear some days
Not as obvious but he's still somewhere
Saying
"You're not good enough"
"You will never be loved"
"Something is, and always will be,
Wrong with you"
"Life is, and always will be,
Tough"
When I hear these things I try to run
But I cannot run from myself

Things I want to say

I hid so much
I've forgotten what it's like to be found
                            - I even hid from myself

Things I want to say

I've spent days in bed paralysed by the emptiness
I've attempted to cry everything undone
But there is nothing left
And still nothing has changed
I have lost count of how many times
The sun has risen
And set
And risen
How many times I have hit rock bottom
And crawled back out
Just to hit it again
I'm not sure I have it in me anymore

Things I want to say

I attempted to leave so many fucking times
But each time, my heart shattered under the pressure
Willing for relief I would return
Maybe this is why I allowed you
To burn me alive
Because something is always better than nothing
right?
Having you there
Even when you are not loving
Is better than not having you at all
I can take the hurt
But not your absence
I know I am chasing a ghost
But does it matter
Because at least I have something

Things I want to say

Loving you is like swimming
But the water disappearing
Before I make it to the deep end

                                       - I can't quite do it

Things I want to say

I made your coal into diamonds
While you made my diamonds into coal
And as each new day passes
I realise your true goal
And as I stop wishing for you to be someone you are
not
Your wishes about me are just starting to rot

Things I want to say

I hope the world gives you strength
Continues to dot your face with those larger than life
smiles
And gives you a high five

I hope the world shows love to you

I hope the world gives you determination
Continues filling your lungs with air
And doesn't rid you of your strong opinions and
stubborn will

More than anything else I hope the world
Deals you better cards
Than the ones it dealt me

Things I want to say

It's not an natural born love story
One where I was made for them
And them for me
It's a recycling of same abuse
Over and fucking over again
And I can't keep letting myself get hurt
We were just not meant to be
And one day I think I'll realise that
I think I have been realising that
And just because they made me
And make an effort with me
And are there sometimes when I cry
Doesn't take away from the fact that
Sometimes those tears are because of them

Things I want to say

Social media memories remind me every year of what
I was doing
1 year
2 years
5 years
Ago
Asks "do you remember what you were doing"
On this date in this year

And most of the time I don't
Most of the time it's a silly picture or a random video
Of me
Of my friends
Of a family day out

But sometimes it's you
Or them
I was listening to a song that I avoid now
Or in a house I no longer view as home
Or messing around with people I don't know anymore

I still look at the pictures
Trying to remember all the good times
Remember the sound of your voice
The smell of our favourite body spray
Just trying to bring every piece of you back into my
head again
And soak up the presence of you being next to me

Social media memories ask if I remember

Things I want to say

What I was doing
On this date in this year
And fuck, I was trying so hard not to

Things I want to say

"Are you okay?"

To put it nicely
I am still sitting on the
Of the clinical looking cold room
Watching someone head banging in the next room
I am looking more and more like them
As each day passes
By that I mean opinions get swallowed back down my throat
By that I mean I am feeling pain
I am not allowed to claim as my own
I can change absolutely nothing
About this situation
But I still go back to that doorway
Embrace them with a hug
Trying to go back to a time
They don't regret

Things I want to say

I'd like to believe that there's this
Other
Version of me
Out there
In there
Somewhere
One who hasn't been hurt
Or seen the pain that I've seen
One whose head wasn't filled with screaming
And fighting
And cheating
Not sat there wondering why she wasn't good enough
For anyone
I'd like to believe that there's this
Other
Version of me
And I often think about what she'd be doing now
Going to a party with her friends on a Saturday night
Talking to her family about music and not stuck in
her head
I hope she never has to feel like giving up
I hope she never has to feel this crazy

Things I want to say

You know how sometimes you aren't aware that you
have a cold
Until your temperature skyrockets
And you wake only being able to breathe out of one
nostril?
Then all of a sudden and all at once
All the symptoms hit you
And you're unable to move and your body feels so
incredibly
Heavy
But a few hours ago you felt completely and utterly
Healthy
I think this is a lot like that
Sometimes I am not aware that there's a part of me
That is still struggling
Until something comes along to remind me
That I am still horribly and overwhelmingly
Broken

Things I want to say

I think people like me better when they experience me less

Because you can appreciate a storm without the need to be in it

And you can observe the sharks without submerging yourself into the sea

What I mean to say is that I am the storm

And I am the shark

You cannot get close without getting hurt

The boats are there to keep YOU safe

Not me

An invisible layer of protection

Because please don't come too near

Oh God, don't come too near

My lack of ability makes the change in closeness too great of a weight to bare

Sometimes I often wonder if it would be better to just not know me at all

Because you can't touch a fire without getting a few burns

Things I want to say

Think positively and you'll be happy
Eat healthy food and you'll feel happy
Change your habits and you'll be a happy person
Go get help
Go get help and talk to someone
Talk to someone?
I AM TALKING TO YOU
I'm trying to tell you I don't know if I will make it out
of this alive
I don't know how to take the voices in my head and
make them fight WITH me
Instead of against me
That I don't know how to go to sleep at night without
feeling suffocated by the bedsheets
I'm trying to tell you that I can't think without
questioning
Everything
But you're looking at me as if I am broken
I am not broken
I do not need you to look at me with despair in your
eyes
As if you know I cannot pick myself up and crawl
back to who I was before
Because I know how to do that
I've done it so many damn times
I am just tired
I'm tired
And I am talking to you
I am trying to show you that this?
This is all I have left to give

Things I want to say

I am asking YOU to help me
I don't want to talk to some stranger who will look at
me
And apologise to me
Tell me they are sorry for my life
Who will tell me that I am strong enough to get
through this
But I do not want to be strong anymore
I am talking to you
But you can't read between the lines

Things I want to say

Please stop telling me that it made me a better person
That going through all of that made me who I am
today
I did not deserve to go through it
It did not carve me into a better individual
I would have been just as compassionate
Just as smart
Just as strong
Had it never happened
I did not deserve to go through it
So please do not say it made me a better person
Because I was just as good before it
Before the day that is now ingrained forever in my
mind
Don't say that it made me who I am today
Because that suggests that it needed to happen
That I deserved it in some way
I did not deserve to go through it
Whilst I am a better person
Strong, resilient, kind
And I have proven that by pushing through
By getting through each day when I saw no way out
I did not deserve to go through it
Those bad times did not change my character
I was all of that
Before it all

Things I want to say

From within the depths of my bones
And with the entirety of my body
I am bone achingly tired
If nothing I do is ever good enough
Then I refuse to begin to even try
I will never be the person you wanted
And I think I've come to terms with it enough
To accept it

Things I want to say

I promise I'm still listening
I'm just a little tired
That is what you said
Because that's what people who care about you do at
1am
They give up their sleep to help you
They lay there sleepy eyed and yawning
Listening to your worries
Staying awake for as long as they can
There are some people that will fill even the darkest of
nights with love
Just to try and save you
There are some people who seem to be made of moon-
dust and sunflowers
You were one of them
Talking about you in the past tense just doesn't make
sense to me
There should be no universe in which your face
doesn't exist
So as my heart breaks into a thousand pieces
And a million tears fall down my cheeks at 1am
As I scream profanities hoping something will bring
you back
I think about the day I last saw your face
Heard your voice
And I know you couldn't speak
But my heart understood what you said
And I know I can't see you now
But I still hear you

Things I want to say

And I promise I'm still listening

So I'm guessing you've heard of that quote about the burning house?
The one that says if you were born into a burning house you think the whole world is on fire, but it's not.

Well I think that's bullshit
Because even a burning house has windows
Even smoke filled windows show some sort of clouded reality
And I knew my house was burning
I knew from the moment I was old enough to know my own mind
That my house was burning
But I could still look through the windows
I could still feel the flames licking at my hair and singeing my skin
Just because I was born into a burning house
Does not mean I didn't know any different

And just because I knew my house was on fire
Does not mean I could stop it
Believe me, I tried
But it takes a team of firefighters to put out even the smallest of fires
And I had no team
I mean, I came close to putting out the fires
But the flames would reignite

Things I want to say

And by that I mean the water I used to put out the
fire
Was a conversation with teachers after one too many
bad nights in my own head
Was a visit to a therapist in which I was taught to
protect ourselves with a fire blanket
By that I mean as soon as they were gone
The flames were allowed to wreak havoc on my house
And they'd burn me even more than before

So I learnt to live with pain
I learnt to cover up the burnt skin and broken heart
If you add oxygen to a fire it makes it worse
So I learnt to stay very still and let the flames rise
around me
I learnt that sometimes a burning house can't be
saved
And that the people who live in it can't escape

So yeah, I think it's bullshit
I knew that my house was burning but I did not think
the whole world was too
I could see through the smoke and look through the
windows
I just couldn't get out the door

Things I want to say

"You carry so much love in your heart"
"You're so kind and caring"
"You have so much to offer the world"
I hear what you're saying
I do
But my brain turns the words into poison
Wraps the toxicity around my heart and rots my organs
That's the thing with compliments
They're hard to swallow when you have not heard them
When you have spent your life learning only of bad people
Love is unfamiliar
Kindness looks strange
It is not to say I do not know what these words mean
I see them in the other people
I see the way that some people sound and look like honey
How their smiles are contagious
And they are surrounded in an aura of love
But I do not see that in me
My head turns every positive into a negative
Every negative into another aching wound
And I so desperately want to believe what I am hearing
But when it comes down to it
In the darkness of the night with only the moon for company
None of it matters

Things I want to say

Because I am not full of love or kindness
I am full of hurt and of pain and nothing can take
that away
"We want to keep you safe"
I am not safe
You cannot take me out of my brain

Things I want to say

I always say I've never felt "at home"
Because I know what that phrase is supposed to mean but
Home does not feel to me, the same way it does to you
Home to you, is somewhere you feel safe and protected
Whereas I grew up with a mind that hated me
It was so messed up that I took the words 'pain' and 'love'
And confused them with each other
I always say I've never felt "at home"
That the reason I'm so obedient - (too scared of conflict)
So easy to please - (too scared to have my own opinions)
Is because I lived in constant fear
Unable to speak
And now I hope I never feel "at home" again

Things I want to say

Sometimes I wonder how much the birth order may
have shaped me
Has being the eldest formed my personality?
Forced me into caretaker even if it isn't actually my
natural ability
I always wondered who I would be
Had I been born somewhere in the middle or even last
Would I still feel responsible for everyone's feelings?
Would I still be the only one who was told not to cry
When I was reminded of what has passed
Who would have grown up alongside my siblings?
Would I still be the person who put everyone else
first?
Would I have finally been able to let that guard
down?
Would I have trusted people more easily?
I wish I didn't have to grow up so fast
Able to play just that little bit longer
And I do still feel guilty for leaving
But
No one prepared me for how bad it would hurt
How being somewhere new would take so much work
I felt like glue
So how could I be happy when I knew everyone else
was suffering
I got told to "put myself first"
But who even am I when not fixing someone's hurt?

Things I want to say

It's complex
But I thought I hated myself
Maybe I still do
But hate's a strong word and doesn't really fit the
mood
I hate what I act like
My actions turned me into who I am
It runs in the family
There's trauma in the bloodline
I got high on nostalgia when I was too young
But it was all pretend
I had this little dreamworld where everything was
different
Cause I thought I was a good kid
Good grades, thought I was gifted
Cause school was a nice place
Where I tried my hardest to hide all the pain
But I hated myself because that's what my mind said
And I felt like a burden so tried to be perfect
Took care of myself till my mind said I couldn't
But it's still complex

Things I want to say

- Revised from 14 years old

People sit there and they judge
They judge on looks, personality, materialistic items
And people have no idea it's happening
There is nothing that can be done to stop it
Sitting there and looking people up and down
They can be so mean
Judging on looks alone
Not someone's life
People who hate other people?
Fuck it, they don't know what you've been through
Nor what you are going through
People can be so mean
Acting all friendly then talking behind your back
Saying they love you then calling you names
Acting like you don't care
Putting a smile on your face
Until you are alone and then the tears don't stop
streaming
Crying until you feel sick
Feeling so broken and you've had enough
You can't stop hurting and feeling shit inside
Acting like you don't care but honestly?
You couldn't care more
People see you
Think they know you
Seeing your fake smile everyday makes them think
that you are happy
But these are the ones that judge you

Things I want to say

The ones that created that fake smile
Make you paranoid, lower your self esteem
You end up feeling gut wrenchingly hurt
All you can think of is when you can let it all out
Standing in front of the mirror
Hating your body, your mind, your personality
You need help and you need it soon
You want to talk but
The only ones you talk to are the ones that have used you
The ones that made you feel the way you do
So who is left?

Things I want to say

- Revised from 13 years old

So let me get something straight
I listen to you whether I want to or not
I help you whether you want it or not
But when I need you?
You just complain
Change conversation topic
Just breeze past it
You know everything about me
What I did, what I went through
It literally spread like wildfire around the school
Do you think of that when I say I need to talk?
You tell me you're there for me and I need to speak
up
So why do you give me the cold shoulder?
Even when you know something serious could be
wrong
Well let's imagine this
One day you didn't want to talk
And I'd had enough?
I tried and tried to get you to listen
And you didn't
So I did do something stupid
And it seriously harmed me
What would you do?
And what if it didn't do any harm?
Would you carry on the way you were?
I could be seriously harmed
All because you couldn't be bothered to care

Things I want to say

- Revised from 13 years old

I cried
And I don't know why
But I cried
Is it because of what happened to me?
Or is it just me?
I hate feeling this way
Wouldn't mind if it was only yesterday
But it's today
And the day before that
I cried and cried till my eyes hurt
I still feel the same though and still want to cry
But I have no tears left
So why would I?
I do though, damn I really do
Cry until I feel sick
Bury my head under the pillow
And block everything out
I want to block you out
I want to block out my life
My smile is fake, feelings are numb
And I've had enough

Things I want to say

- Revised from 14 years old

My younger life was amazing
I had fun and played in the snow
Went to the beach and had fights over crayons
My imagination went wild
I could be whatever I wanted
My younger life was amazing
I had cuddles and kisses
And snuggles and wishes
Ribena was our red wine
And banana's could be innocently eaten
Parties were in the middle of the afternoon
And pass the parcel was the best
Not spin the bottle
My younger life was amazing
Everyone was my best friend
And we called each other cute nicknames
School was fun
Not tense and full of bullies
My younger life was amazing
Computers were only for paint
A bed was for one, not two
Unless it was top and tail
Boys were off limits, girls were never bitchy
My younger life was amazing
Except this is a lie

Things I want to say

- Revised from 15 years old

I'm lying here thinking I'm worthless
Because you used me, abused me
Who the fuck would do that?
Why did I let you?
It's disgusting
You're disgusting
Yet you're free to roam this world
While I'm here
Miles away from you but yet somehow still with you
I'm trapped in this circular room
With nowhere to go
No safe places to be
All thanks to you I'm living in a nightmare
Whilst you're all living out your dreams
I'm sitting here
Tied to a bed that's getting no sleep
I'm trapped in this circular room
All because you abused me, used me
You're talking to me
Saying I'm worthless
Saying it's my fault
And I lay there letting you manipulate me
Because I'm starting to believe it
I'm trapped in this circular room
I'm hurting myself because of you
I hate what you've done to me
But I'm still trapped in this circular room
Called my mind and it's spinning out of control

Things I want to say

- Revised from 15 years old

Why did you do that to her?
You gave up on her
And then you wonder why she doesn't want anything
to do with you
Maybe it's because you put your boyfriend before her
Or maybe it's because you abused her
She went on to have a better life, or so she thought
But yet again, people took her for granted
She'd had enough
Maybe, just maybe, if you were there
Things might have been different
She would have a big family, wouldn't feel so shit
about herself
If you were there to help her
She might have had a better life
But you just didn't care
Hardly ever saw her
Hardly ever rang her
Forgot her birthdays
She thought you hated her
She grew up and then you wanted to know her
But it was too late
She followed in your footsteps
And my childhood was then hers
So I guess "the apple never rots too far from the tree"

Things I want to say

- Revised from 14 years old

Who the fuck do you think you are?
You say you love me
Then say you hate me
You give me cuddles to pick me up
Just to push me down again
And I've had enough
Who the fuck do you think you are?
Using me like this
You just don't really care
You don't care about how I feel
You just want to abuse me
I hate the fact that you don't see what you are doing
Who the fuck do you think you are?
Walking into my life like you don't give a shit
Maybe if you stopped once in a while
You might see my emotions
The raw pain that only I feel
If you just stopped and asked
Then things might have been different
My plans might have changed
Who the fuck do you think you are?
You think you're all it
Yet everybody hates you
You have wasted your time if you think I'll give you a
second chance
So who the fuck do you think you are?

Things I want to say

I want to stop hearing "oh, it'll get better"
Even if it did, I would still have the scars from my
pain
Even if it did, I still wouldn't be able to love myself
Even if it did, I would still be too scared to look in a
mirror
The pain knows me better than anyone else does
The pain used to be my most loyal friend
I can't remember a time where I wasn't searching for
the light
Just to find it was from a source that died an eternity
ago
So no, it doesn't feel like it gets better
It feels harder everyday
I can hear my heartbeat echo in my empty chest
In this body I've neglected
It hasn't gotten any better,
But please,
Tell me it will stop getting worse

Things I want to say

This year has not been the year in which
I repaired my brain
And emptied it of all the hateful shit
It has not been the year in which I started my first job
Or published a book
I did not become a household name
This year has not been the year in which
I have travelled the world
And found THE place I want to live
It has not been the year in which I found THE one
Got married, had kids
And had every day full of fun
This year has not been the year in which
I have forgotten all that has happened
And become someone that other people are inspired
by
It has not been the year in which I got everything I
wanted done
Haven't fulfilled all my new year's resolutions
But I didn't do that the year before
And probably won't in the years to come

Things I want to say

If I was in a fairytale
I would eat all the poisoned apples
And leave one shoe to every pair I own
In every location I go
I would stop cutting my hair
Grow it long enough for you to climb
I would happily never speak again
And stay put on my island
If I was in a fairytale
I would choose not to have a gift
And stay in the jungle
I would do all of this if it meant you wouldn't hurt me
If I was in a fairytale I'd have a happy ending

Things I want to say

You can move a thousand miles away
And create a whole new group of friends
But you cannot get rid of the problems in your brain

To wholeheartedly change your life
You need to move inside yourself
And keep the friends who show you love
You need to learn to love yourself
Accept the help to heal the trauma and the deep
conditioning
From your internal demons

You cannot run away from your brain
But making internal changes will
In turn
Make external ones

Things I want to say

I pull at memories
Like I pulled at my loose teeth
So the tooth fairy would pay me a visit
And I bleed from the memories
Like the blood that poured from my mouth
Reminding me that actions have consequences
But I never learnt
I continued pulling on my loose teeth
Just like I continue pulling from bad memories
When will I learn that there is no fairy
To reward me for my consequences

Things I want to say

I visit your grave twice a day
I'm sorry
I'm sorry
I sleep there every night
I spend hours smashing up your grave
Then hours putting it back together
I grow your favourite flowers
Then let them grow wild
Just so I can strangle the weeds
I trace our names
Mine is deeper than yours
I trace the end dates of our lives
Mine ends differently
Our ghosts sit besides me
We are laughing, we are singing
And we are happy,
But I have never felt so alone

Things I want to say

I've forever been the girl to say I can do this
Even with mascara rolling down my cheeks
And this is how I will always be
Until the day that I die
Because the only person we can truly count on is
yourself
No one else is going to piece me back together
And when I fall down I have 2 choices
I can pick up the shards and puzzle them back
together up or
I can let myself drown
That's the brain I live in
That's how it has always been
So I can do this
People can try and help me but I push them away
before I even know I'm doing it
Because when you rely on somebody once
You'll form it into a habit
And the next time I need them
They'll have disappeared
And I'll be the one left in pain
But don't fret
Every time I fall I have to get back up
I'll never need anyone to piece me together
Because I'll forever be the girl who says I can do this
Even with mascara rolling down my cheeks

Things I want to say

I may have never been able to meet you
Or hold you
Or comfort you
But you are in everything I do
I hear you in the songs that sing me to sleep at 1am
I see you in old baby pictures as though you're
looking back at me
I hear you in the laughs of my siblings when they're
being tickled
I see you in the petals of the flowers growing through
the cracks in the path
I feel you in my heart when I think of what your name
would have been
It will always be my favourite
I see you in all the art at my favourite coffee shop
I hear you calling for me in the dark of the night when
you need me
I may never have been able to meet you, but you're
always there
I may never have been able to hear you but I can
always hear my soul missing yours
I may never be able to know who you would have
turned into but I know
No matter what
You were going to be perfect
Because you were wholeheartedly mine

Things I want to say

If I could
I'd have my future set in stone
I keep being told that I must be on this earth to help
others
I've known this forever
But my soul is tired,
I have been here so many times before
I was told that I must have been a doctor, or a
therapist or a teacher in a past life
Sometimes I hate this
Sometimes I want to scream and shout that I don't
want to help others
Anymore
That this is not who I am
And sometimes I find comfort in this fact
Sometimes I feel that if I did not help others
I would not be me anymore
And sometimes I wonder if I should be sad
Because it's astrologically pre-determined to pour
more into people
Than I even own in my cup
Is it some cruel trick?
Always the artist, but never the art?
Is the only good thing about me to recognise the good
in others
Maybe I will always be the one to love harder than I
will ever be loved
But what a privilege it is
To love

Things I want to say

I fall down on the floor
Maybe curl up into a ball
Start to hyperventilate
And I'll try to breathe in and out
In and out
Counting 1...2...3...4
But I can't yet get my lungs to work right
I hear the caring voices repeating my name
But they're so far in the distance that I can't focus on
them
I fall further and further into the past
They wait patiently
For me to open my eyes and reassure them that I am
okay
They make small talk and rub my arms
Remind me that I am safe
To try and calm me down or bring me back to the
present
But I sit there
I sit there and I wonder who I am. What I did wrong.
When will this stop? Where am I supposed to go from
here? Why is this happening? How can I keep
Going?
Without any warning things changed overnight
My body changed and my mind stopped working the
right way
I have all the correct parts and pieces
But they just don't work collaboratively
Or maybe they just don't know how
I don't know

Things I want to say

But I'm waiting for my lungs to work so I can breathe
again
Waiting for my eyes to open so I can see the real
world again
Maybe 5 minutes pass by
And then after a few seconds
After that
It's raced to 15 minutes
And I try so hard to come out
To move my fingers and open my eyes
To get out of this cycle that I seem to find myself in
But it never works
And finally
After an eternity of not being able to respond to
anyone around me
My breathing slows
The world comes back into view and I stop shaking
I get up and I push through my day and I do that
One baby step at a time

Things I want to say

I want to burn the feel of you from my brain
Delete the memories that you left behind
I want to ruin the house that you made from my
bones
I want back the pieces of my soul that you stole
I want them back
The missing pieces are leaving a hole
A hole that makes it feel as though I am falling into
myself
I gave you what you wanted as soon as you wanted
Straight away
So why can't I have the shards of me back NOW
I do not want to be a fragment of a person because
you stole the other pieces of me
You created a person that I do not recognise when I
look at my reflection
I catch myself when walking past
And have to take another glance
Inspect myself from all angles and wonder what
happened to me
What happened to me?
When did I became so distorted
So unrecognisable
I just want to be the person I was
Before you stole from me

Things I want to say

The pain that you handed me has emptied me
I'm exhausted
It's left me feeling unaligned and not sure of the right
turning
It's hard to get out of bed
There's mourning in the morning
The sunlight has risen again
But my thoughts are dark and haunted
Sometimes I think upon the reason for this intrusion
All the awful words you threw my way
Shadow person, did you really mean them?
I'm unsure on who you are now
And I still don't know the reason
You're a shadow of the person
That I once both loved and found love in
Tell me, shadow person
Where did you hide the good ones?
Or were you here all along but pushed into the corner
You cut me when I held your face
Your rose petals became rose thorns
Why the change of heart
Why have you deceived me and left me torn
I built a bridge between us just to watch you burn it
to the ground
Your smiling so unsettling as I listen to the sound
Of melting metal and concrete crumbling
I prayed for a cloud overfilled with rain to wash away
my tears
And kill the fire
But

Things I want to say

Not one cloud was sent to
Stop the spiteful service
No roaring tsunami
To wash away the sins
I know fire is to be hot
But I was so cold
Just hit with absolute devastation
And then I realised
That you were not taught what actual love is
All the pain that you handed me has emptied me
I'm exhausted
It's left me feeling unaligned and not sure of the right
turning
Shadow person, let me know, with your destruction
and your laughter
Have you had your fill of fun?
Will this make you calmer?

Things I want to say

I am on a train
Or a bus
Or any form of transport really
The people behind me laugh
And I'm pretty sure they're laughing at me
Maybe it's because my dress is too tight
Fuck, my dress is definitely too tight
Or maybe it's because they think I'm strange
We arrive at our destination and I say thank you to
the staff
They just stare at me
And I think maybe I didn't actually say it
Or maybe it's because they think I'm strange
I am walking down the road
Music on to stop the sound of the cars
Counting to regulate my breathing
I see someone I know, or once knew and I smile
They carry on walking
Maybe it's because I did something wrong
Fuck, I definitely did something wrong
Or maybe they just think I'm strange
Fuck, I hope I'm definitely not strange

Things I want to say

I'm actually okay thank you
I do not want a house
I do not want pristine furniture and cold coloured
walls
Nor do I want all my possessions hidden
Like I hide all the messy parts of me
I wish for the bed to be the safest place I can be
And I want belongings spread across every surface
Showing signs of a good life lived
And if I must have a welcome sign
I want it to say incompleteness before it
And it WILL almost definitely be incomplete
So no
I do not want a house
But I do wish for a home

Things I want to say

Sometimes I have this intrusive thought that questions why
They chose me
And wonders if they'd be happier with somebody else
Somebody who doesn't struggle as much
And when they ask what they can do to help
I wish I could give an answer
I want to not feel this way
I wish that I didn't feel such a burden
I want to not have that guilt everyday
Because I don't really know what to do with it
One day they're going to decide that it's too much
And leave
But I want them to know I am trying so hard
As hard as I can to protect them
Because I know it's not their job to fix me
And I know they want to
So I want them to promise me
That if I ever get too much
If they ever need some space
It doesn't matter how bad I feel that day
They will promise to ask for it

Things I want to say

I long for something I have never had
Or for something I HAVE had
In the past
I long for what every teenager has dreamt of
I want love
I want the movie kinda love
The kiss on the doorstep at 1am kinda love
I want someone to be addicted to the thought of me
For them to turn bright red just from hearing my
name
I want someone to hold me
And comfort me
To lay in bed next to me
And whisper cheesy sweet nothings in my ear
I just want to be wanted

Things I want to say

We may not be lovers
But we are
In love
It's what everyone says about us
Sometime they question if we are actually
Dating
And other people stare at us
Because they want to share a space with someone
And actually
Truly
Share it
Not just coexist next to someone
They want our
Inside jokes
Our
Magnetic connection
We are two halves
Of a whole
We share thoughts
Finish each other's sentences
Effortlessly mirror each other's movements
And we both forget what we want to say but with the
other we are fluent
We said we'll get married
If we were both single at 35
We may not be together
And we never will be
What we have is strictly platonic
But we are oh so in love just as we should be

Things I want to say

How many times has someone dismissed our pain
And essentially said
Get over it?
Sticks and stones will break our bones
But words
Can break our souls
Words can be permanent
Inked into the skin like a bad tattoo
Words have taken away trust
Dimmed the light that we once had
We've gone from "this is who I am"
To
"This is who I was"
We've been told that words won't actually kill us
But what they meant to say is
"Words won't PHYSICALLY kill you"
But they can kill parts of us
We didn't know existed
"Sticks and stones may break your bones but words
will never hurt you"
NO
Sticks and stones may break my bones but words will
cause more damage

Things I want to say

Why did no one teach us
That people are not homes
You cannot find peace in someone else
People are not a permanent structure
They are not a structure that stays the same
For people are ever changing beings
We ebb and flow through life
Like the ocean upon the shore
We take our experiences and let them influence us
For good or bad
We go from bad to good, from hot to cold
Just like the seasons do
Houses are not found in other people
They are not found within unrealistic ideals
Homes do have heartbeats
But this is found inside ourselves
When we begin to heal

Things I want to say

I'll never be who I was before
Before the weight of this world
Became too hard to bare
This is not inherently a bad thing
For now?
Now I am more kind
More caring
And that's not to say I wasn't that before
But now I am also more selfish
And that's okay
You cannot pour from an empty cup

Things I want to say

I was once told
If you do not change
You cannot grow
And I took that and threw it away
Who were they to tell me that?
I have always been the same
I like consistency
And I thrive off routine
I had no want
Nor need
For change
But after that seed was planted
A thought started to grow
It rooted down within my brain
And started sprouting
Very slow
And after a while I started to realise
An ocean wave meets the shore
Despite it being
Sent away
And the leaves still grow upon the trees despite the
seasons change
The world is always changing so why was I afraid?
And change is okay when done in the right way
And if I don't change and grow each day
Opportunities will almost always
Never come my way

Things I want to say

I can see the braveness in your mind
I feel how hard you fight
This life has been oh so cruel
But baby, please don't cry
I can see how hard this is for you
But look back at where you came from
Hold my hand and feel my touch
Your eyes are oh so brightsome
I can see how full your heart is
How much you can achieve
So baby, please don't cry
Lift your head up and believe

Things I want to say

I didn't know at what point
God would call your names
I thought of you in life
And in death I'll do the same
It broke my heart to lose you
I thought I'd be alone
But a piece of me went with you
When you left for home
You left us some questionable memories
Some I like to hide
And I may never see you
But you're always by my side
Our family tree has been broken
And it has never felt the same
But one by one we'll join you
And be family once again

Things I want to say

Sometimes I think to myself
"Doesn't life happen in a funny way?"
At any moment in time we could make one split
decision
A decision that could lead to the best moment in our
lives
Or the worst
A decision that could mend our heart
Or break it
A decision that could give us everything we want
Or rip it from our palms
And this sort of thought
Makes me want to grip life with two hands
And never let it go

Things I want to say

Let me tell you a story
And explain why I didn't stop
I fought through every battle
Until my head started to throb
I walked through each flame
And put out every fire
The stars hold all my wishes
About building me up higher
A fear had started to settle
Right inside my bones
Telling me if I stay still
I'll always be alone
But my fighting has gotten slower
And I look back at where I've been
Just to find the gaps
Where people have been mean
So I've began to start doing
Things I want to do
And I've started singing
Along to my favourite tunes
I've began seeing
The sights I want to see
But most importantly
I've become my own human being

Things I want to say

If you say the same thing over and over
Again and again
It starts to lose all it's meaning
I feel like life is a lot like that
If you keep doing the same thing over and over
Again and again
Then you'll never learn
That you can mend

       - Make positive changes

Things I want to say

Dear readers
I love you
Yes
You with the fragile mind and soft heart
Don't forget how brave you are
How strong you are
You have survived so much in this life
If you cry at another's pain
If your mind squishes under pressure
If your souls melt
After the thought of someone's hurt
Please stay like this
Please do not let the burdens of this earth
Turn you into stone

Printed in Great Britain
by Amazon

22869795R00057